Wolfgang Amadeus Mozart

COSÌ FAN TUTTE

in Full Score

Dover Publications, Inc.
New York

Aus rechtlichen Gründen darf dieses Werk nicht im Gebiet
der Bundesrepublik Deutschland und West-Berlin angeboten
und/oder verkauft werden.

For legal reasons this title cannot be offered or sold in
Federal Republic of Germany and West Berlin.

This Dover edition, first published in 1983, is an unabridged republication of the
edition by Georg Schünemann and Kurt Soldan, with German translation of the vocal
text by Georg Schünemann, originally published by C. F. Peters, Leipzig, n.d. (publication number 11467; editorial matter dated "Summer 1941"). In the present edition
all the preliminary matter and the Editors' Commentary (*Revisionsbericht*), originally in
German, appear in a new English translation specially prepared by Stanley Appelbaum.

Manufactured in the United States of America
Dover Publications, Inc., 180 Varick Street, New York, N.Y. 10014

Library of Congress Cataloging in Publication Data

Mozart, Wolfgang Amadeus, 1756–1791.
    [Così fan tutte. German & Italian]
    Così fan tutte.

    Opera.
    German and Italian words.
    Libretto by Lorenzo Da Ponte.
    Originally edited by Georg Schünemann and Kurt Soldan ; German translation of
libretto by Schünemann ; editorial matter translated into English by Stanley Appelbaum.
    Reprint. Originally published: Leipzig : C. F. Peters, 1941.
    1. Operas—Scores. I. Da Ponte, Lorenzo, 1749–1838. II. Title.
M1500.M84C542   1983   83-5140
ISBN 0-486-24528-4

COSÌ FAN TUTTE

COMIC OPERA IN TWO ACTS TEXT BY LORENZO DA PONTE MUSIC BY W. A. MOZART	DRAMMA GIOCOSO IN DUE ATTI POESIA DI LORENZO DA PONTE MUSICA DI W. A. MOZART
## CHARACTERS	## PERSONAGGI

FIORDILIGI }	ladies from Ferrara, sisters, residing in	{ Soprano	FIORDILIGI }	Dame Ferrarese e sorelle abitanti in	{ Soprano
DORABELLA)	Naples.................	(Soprano	DORABELLA)	Napoli..................	(Soprano
GUGLIELMO,	officer, in love with Fiordiligi................	Baritone	GUGLIELMO,	Ufficiale, amante di Fiordiligi................	Baritono
FERRANDO,	officer, in love with Dorabella..................	Tenor	FERRANDO,	Ufficiale, amante di Dorabella..................	Tenore
DESPINA,	chambermaid of the ladies....................	Soprano	DESPINA,	Cameriera delle dame....................	Soprano
DON ALFONSO,	an old philosopher.........	Bass	DON ALFONSO,	vecchio Filosofo...........	Basso

Soldiers, servants, sailors, wedding guests, populace.	Soldati, Servitori, Marinari, Convitati alle nozze, Popolo.
The action takes place in Naples.	La scena si finge in Napoli.

Composed in 1789/90. First performed at the National Court Theater
in Vienna on January 26, 1790, under the composer's direction.

INSTRUMENTATION

2 Flutes (Flauti) – 2 Oboes (Oboi) – 2 Clarinets (Clarinetti) – 2 Bassoons (Fagotti)
2 Horns (Corni) – 2 Trumpets (Trombe) – 2 Kettledrums (Timpani) – Violins (Violini) I & II
Violas (Viole) – Cellos (Violoncelli) – Basses (Contrabassi)

ON STAGE

1 Snare Drum (Tamburo militare)

Contents

Preface

In a time of extreme financial distress, when Mozart was barely managing to contend with his pressing cares, Emperor Joseph II commissioned him to write a new comic opera. The librettist was to be Lorenzo da Ponte, who was to write an effective script in accordance with a given poetic idea. Da Ponte called the new opera *Così fan tutte ossia la scuola degli amanti*. Mozart began at once on the composition, for which he was promised 200 ducats. By December 31, 1789, he had made such great progress that he was able to play excerpts from the score for his friends Puchberg and Haydn. With the new year, rehearsals began, and on January 26, 1790 the first performance of the work (with the German subtitle "So machen sie's oder die Schule der Liebhaber") took place at the National Theater in Vienna. The cast was as follows:

Fiordiligi	dame Ferrarese	Sgrn. Ferraresi
Dorabella	e sorelle	del Bene
	abitanti in Napoli	Sgrn. L. Villeneuve
Guglielmo, ufficiale, amante di Fiordiligi		Sgr. Benucci
Ferrando, ufficiale, amante di Dorabella		Sgr. Calvesi
Despina, cameriera delle dame		Sgrn. Bussani
Don Alfonso, vecchio filosofo		Sgr. Bussani

For the first time, Da Ponte's work for Mozart was not based on a firm, well-known model as in the case of *Figaro* and *Don Giovanni*. He had to shape his material freely. In order to create stageworthy and humorous scenes, he adhered to the most popular devices of comic opera. He adopted disguises and mistaken identities as springboards of the action, and from *opera buffa* he added the familiar types of the notary and the physician, the maid experienced in life and love, and the aristocratic, worldly nobleman. Women and men, as in *Figaro*, were allotted time-honored sentiments concerning the faithlessness of the opposite sex. They were asked to sing about the Eumenides, Penelope, Cyclops, Charon and Aesop in the style of grand opera. These parodies and comic situations with poisoning, magical cure and crisscross love were meant to cloak the daring aspect of the plot.

Mozart fleshed out the story with the full melodic and dramatic power of his years of mastery. The large number of ensembles gave him rich opportunity to heighten or resolve the dramatic conflicts, to deepen and ennoble the characters. Gravity and fun, truth and appearance, lies and deception are illumined by a magical glow that transfigures them all. A subtle veil of light musical irony is spread over the entire proceedings.

No opera has been readapted as often and as thoroughly as *Così Fan Tutte*. The libretto has stirred up moralists, playwrights, musicians and poets, who in numerous suggested improvements have altered, turned around or completely reshaped the action. Some introduced magical elements, some replaced the fiancés with friends, some had the men duped by the women in their turn, some finally tried totally different texts. These German revisions begin right after the first production. The versions *Eine macht's wie die andre oder die Schule der Liebhaber* (1792) and Bretzner's *Weibertreue oder die Mädchen sind von Flandern* (1794) received numerous performances. Treitschke made two attempts with the material, once with *Mädchentreue* (1805), then with *Die Zauberprobe* (1814). Berlin saw Herclots' *Die verfängliche Wette* in 1820 and Louis Schneider's *So machen es alle* in 1846. In his adaptation of 1860, which used a fluid and skillful translation, Eduard Devrient reintroduced the recitative. In 1909 Karl Scheidemantel substituted a text based on Calderón's *La dama duende*. But all of these experiments and many similar ones were failures. It was only the restoration of the original form in the version by Karl Niese (1871) that gave new impetus to the opera. After it had been freely adapted by Hermann Levi on the basis of Devrient and Niese, in more recent years (1936) Siegfried Anheisser once more presented a literal translation.

The present version is based on tradition and on the original text. All older translations, among which those of Devrient, Bernhard von Gugler (*Sind sie treu?*) and Karl Niese are outstanding, were taken into account and compared with the original text. Every note of Mozart's, every turn of verbal and musical phrase, was preserved intact. Whatever lasting contribution was made during the history of the opera lives on in the new translation. Whatever was superseded, off the track or contrary to Mozart's music was reshaped with the strictest regard to Mozart's own manuscript.

In the editing of the score, the conductor Kurt Soldan helped me immeasurably with his great knowledge and his exactitude in all matters of textual criticism. I would like to express my thanks to him here too.

Berlin, Summer 1941

GEORG SCHÜNEMANN

COSÌ FAN TUTTE

Ouvertura

W. A. Mozart
(1756–1791)

4

6

7

8

13

14

ERSTER AKT
Kaffeehaus
Erste Szene
[Ferrando. Don Alfonso. Guglielmo.]

ATTO PRIMO
Bottega di Caffè
Scena I
[Ferrando, Don Alfonso, Guglielmo.]

№ 1. Terzetto

20

Recitativo

attacca il Terzetto No 2

24

Nº 2. Terzetto

28

attacca il Terzetto Nº 3

Nº 3. Terzetto

30

36

Verwandlung
Garten am Meeresstrand

Zweite Szene
Fiordiligi und Dorabella [jede ein Bild betrachtend,
welches sie an der Seite hängend tragen].

Mutazione
Giardino sulla spiaggia [del mare].

Scena II
Fiordiligi e Dorabella [che guardano un ritratto
che lor pende al fianco].

Nº 4. Duetto

Recitativo

Fiordiligi

An die-sem schönen Morgen fühl ich neu mich be-lebt zu tau-send Scherzen: In mei-nen A-dern fühl heu-te ich ein
Mi par, che sta-mat-ti-na vo-len-tie-ri fa-rei la paz-za-rel-la: ho un cer-to fo-co, un cer-to piz-zi-

[4] **Fiordiligi / Dorabella**

Prickeln meines Blutes... und kommt erst mein Guglielmo...macht ich gerne mit ihm gleich ei-nen Scherz! Ich muß ge-stehen, auch in
cor en-tro le ve-ne... quan-do Gu-gliel-mo vie-ne... se sa-pessi che bur-la gli vo far! Per dir-ti il ve-ro, qual-che

[8] **Dorabella / Fiordiligi**

mir regt sich mächtig ein un-ge-wohntes Feuer: Ich möchte schwören, daß wir bald am Al-ta-re Hymens stehen. Laß dei-ne
co-sa di nuo-vo anch' io nell' al-ma provo: io giu-re-re-i, che lon-ta-ne non siam da-gli I-me-ne-i. Dam-mi la

[12] **Fiordiligi / Dorabella**

Hand sehn, ich will dir prophe-zeien: Sieh dieses B hier, und hier ein H, was heißt das? Bal-di-ge Hochzeit. Ich hätte nichts da-
ma-no: io vo-glio a-stro-lo-gar-ti: uh che bell' Em-me, e que-sto è un Pì: va be-ne: matrimonio pre-sto. Af-fè che ci a-vrei

[17] **Fiordiligi / Dorabella**

gegen! Auch ich würd gar nicht bös sein. Doch was ist nur ge-sche-hen, un-sre Rit-ter sind immer noch nicht hier? Es wird schon
gusto! Ed io non ci a-vrei rabbia. Ma che dia-vol vuol dir che i no-stri spo-si ri-tar-da-no a ve-nir? Son già le

Dritte Szene   ## Scena III

Die Vorigen. Don Alfonso.   Le suddette e Don Alfonso.

[21] **Fiordiligi Dorabella / Don Alfonso / Dorab.**

spät... Dort sind sie. Nein, sie sind's nicht, es ist Alfonso, ihr alter Freund. Willkommen, Signor Don Al-fonso. Meine Damen. Was
se-i... Ec-co-li. Non son es-si: è Don Alfonso, l'a-mi-co lor. Ben ven-ga il Signor Don Al-fon-so. Ri-ve-ri-sco. Cos'

Nº 5. Aria

Recitativo

segue Quintetto No 6

Vierte Szene
[Die Vorigen. Ferrando und Guglielmo (in Reisekleidern).]

Scena IV
[I suddetti; Ferrando, Guglielmo (in abito da viaggio).]

Nº 6. Quintetto

Guglielmo

Schwankend nah ich, die Schrit-te za-gen, kaum daß mich die Fü-ße
Sen - to, o Di - o, che que - sto pie-de è re - stio nel gir - le a-

Ferrando

Mei - ne Lip-pen, sie ver-sa-gen, ach, kein Wort bring ich her-vor.
Il mio l'ab-bro pal - pi - tan-te, non può det - to pro-nun-ziar.

Don Alfonso
Droht das
Nei mo-

tra-gen.
van-te.

54

Recitativo*)

attacca il Duettino Nº 7

Nº 7. Duettino*⁾

*Often omitted.

62

Recitativo

segue Coro Nº 8

Fünfte Szene

[Die Vorigen. Soldaten. Männer und Frauen.]
[Von fern hört man einen Marsch; eine Barke legt am Ufer an.]

Scena V

[I suddetti, Soldati, Uomini e Donne.]
[Marcia militare in qualche distanza; arriva una barca alla sponda.]

№ 8. Coro

64

O,wie schön,Soldat zu sein,   o,wie schön,Soldat zu sein!   Ein Soldat hat nie zu
Bel- la vi - ta mi- li- tar,   bel- la vi - ta mi-li- tar!   O - gni dì si cangia

O,wie schön,Soldat zu sein,   o,wie schön,Soldat zu sein!   Ein Soldat hat nie zu
Bel- la vi - ta mi- li- tar,   bel- la vi - ta mi-li- tar!   O - gni dì si cangia

66

Recitativo

segue Quintetto Nº 9

Nº 9. Quintetto [e Coro]

4
a 2
Fag.
4
I
Viol.
II
Viola
Fiordiligi
Fi.
schwör... mir's... o... mein... Ge - lieb - ter... sei ge -
giu - - ra mi... vi - ta... mi - a... sii co -
Do.
mir... schrei - be... mir... ver - sprich... mir's...
tu... scri - - vi - - mi... se... puo - i...
Ferrando
Fe.
Ja... si - cher... ja... si - cher... du... Teu - re...
Sii... cer - ta... sii... cer - ta... o... ca - ra...
G.
zwei - fle... nicht... o... zwei - fle... nicht... Ge - lieb - te...
du - bi - tar... non... du - bi - tar... mio be - ne...
Don Alfonso
D.A.
(Ich ster - be noch vor Lachen, ich ster - be noch vor Lachen.)
(Io cre - po se non ri - do, io cre - po se non ri - do.)
Vc.
Cb.
8
I
Viol.
II
Viola
Fi.
treu mir al - lein.
stan - te a me sol.
Dorabella
Do.
Wah - re die Treu - - - - - e!
Ser - ba - ti fi - - - - - - do!
Ferrando
Fe.
Ad -
Ad -
Vc.
Cb.

70

Maestoso

[Die beiden D a m e n bleiben unbeweglich am Meeresstrand zurück; die Barke entfernt sich unter dem Schall der Trommeln]
[Le amanti restano immobili sulla sponda del mare; la barca allontanasi tra suon di tamburi]

O, wie schön, Soldat zu sein, o, wie schön, Soldat zu sein! Ein Sol-dat hat nie zu sor-gen, darbt er
Bel-la vi-ta mi-li-tar, bel-la vi-ta mi-li-tar! O-gni dì si can-gia lo-co, og-gi

heute, schwelgt er morgen, bald zu Land, bald auf der See. Bei Trompe-tenschall und Pfeifenklang, bei dem
molto, do-man po-co, o-ra in ter-ra ed or sul mar. Il fra-gor di trom-be e pif-fe-ri; lo spa-

74

№ 10. Terzettino

78

Siebente Szene
Don Alfonso (allein).

Scena VII
Don Alfonso (solo).

Recitativo

Don Alfonso:
Ich bin kein schlech-ter Schau-spie-ler, schon gut so: Zum Ren-dez-vous er-war-ten mich die Freun-de, die für
Non son cat-ti-vo co-mi-co, va be-ne: al con-cer-ta-to lo-co i due cam-pio-ni di Ci-

Mars und für Ve-nus wie zwei Hel-den sich schla-gen; rasch oh-ne Zau-dern will ich zu ih-nen ei-len... welch Ge-
prigna,e di Mar-te mi sta-ran-no at-ten-den-do; or sen-za in-du-gio, rag-giun-ger-li con-vie-ne... quan-te

ba-ren, welch ü-ber-trieb-ner Jammer... de-sto bes-ser für mich, sie fal-len de-sto schneller: Wer wie sie sich ge-bär-det, pflegt am
smor-fie... quan-te buf-fo-ne-ri-e... tan-to me-glio per me, cadran più fa-cil-men-te: que-sta raz-za di gen-te è la più

schnell-sten sei-nen Sinn zu ver-än-dern. Ihr ar-men To-ren, schon habt ihr die Ze-chi-nen halb ver-
pre-sta a can-giar-si d'u-mo-re. Oh po-ve-ri-ni, per fem-mi-na gio-car cen-to zec-

80

segue Scena VIII

Verwandlung

[Vornehmes Zimmer mit mehreren Sitzgelegenheiten und einem Tischchen.
Drei Türen: Zwei zur Seite, eine in der Mitte.]

Achte Szene

[Despina (im Begriff, Schokolade zuzubereiten).]

Mutazione

[Camera gentile con diverse sedie; un tavolino,
tre porte: due laterali, una di mezzo.]

Scena VIII

[Despina (che sta facendo il cioccolate).]

Recitativo

82

Neunte Szene

Die Vorige. Fiordiligi und Dorabella
[stürzen mit verzweifelten Gebärden herein;
Despina bietet auf einem Tablett die Schokolade an].

Scena IX

La suddetta; Fiordiligi e Dorabella
[ch'entrano disperatamente;
Despina presenta il cioccolate sopra una guantiera].

segue Recitativo Istromentato

segue l'Aria di Dorabella Nº 11

Nº 11. Aria

61
Fl.
Clar. in B
Fag.
Cor. in Es
Viol.
I
II
Viola
Do.
das Herz mir bre - chen, das Herz mir bre - chen,
d'a - mor fu - ne - sto, d'a - mor fu - ne - sto,
Vc.
Cb.
66
a 2
dann, Eu - me - ni - den, sollt ihr mich rä - chen, wenn bang mein
da - rò all' Eu - me - ni - di se vi - va re - sto col suo - no or -

94

Recitativo

attacca subito l'Aria di Despina Nº 12

Nº 12. Aria

stehn. Sie lie-ben nichts in uns als ihr Ver-gnü - gen, und sie ver-ach-ten uns,wennwir er - lie - gen, o, den Bar-
tà. _In noi non a-ma-no che il lor di - let - to, poi ci dis-pre-gia-no, ne-gan-ci af-fet - to, nè val da'_

ba - ren ist Mit-leid so fern, o, den Bar-ba - ren ist Mit-leid so fern, Mit - leid so fern,
bar - ba - ri chie-der pie - tà, nè val da' bar-ba - ri chie-der pie - tà, chie - der pie - tà,

Mitleid so fern.
chie-der pie-tà.

Laßt uns mit glei-chem Geld je-ne be-zah-len, die uns die Ru-he so grausam oft
Pa-ghiam, o fem-mi-ne, d'ugual mo-ne-ta que-sta ma-le-fi-ca raz-za in-dis-

stahlen, liebt nur zum Zeitvertreib, liebt nur zum Spaß, liebt nur zum Zeit-vertreib, liebt nur zum Spaß,
cre-ta; a-miam per co-mo-do, per va-ni-tà, a-miam per co-mo-do, per va-ni-tà,

Zehnte Szene
Don Alfonso (allein). Dann Despina.

Scena X
Don Alfonso (solo), poi Despina.

Recitativo

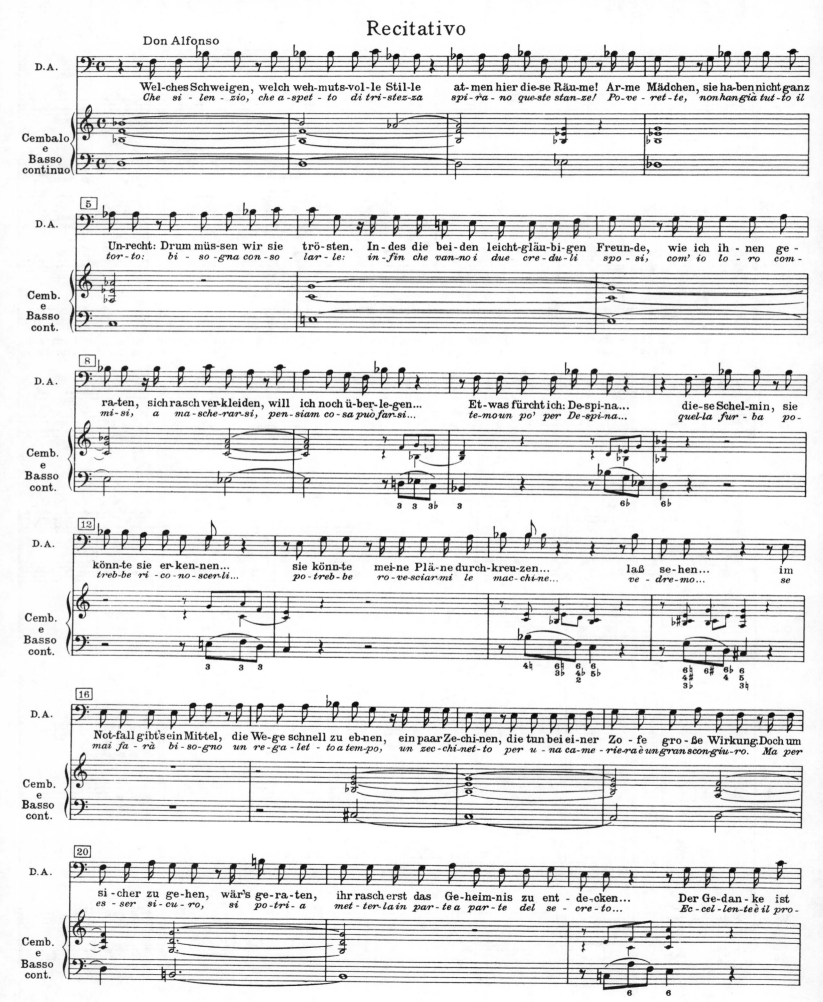

attacca il Sestetto [Nº 13]

Elfte Szene

[Die Vorigen. Ferrando. Guglielmo.
Dann Fiordiligi und Dorabella.]

[Don Alfonso läßt die beiden Liebhaber eintreten]

Scena XI

[I suddetti, Ferrando, Guglielmo;
poi Fiordiligi e Dorabella.]

[Don Alfonso fa entrargli amanti]

Nº 13. Sestetto

108

115

119

123

Recitativo

segue Stromentato

41
Allegro
Viol. I
Viol. II
Viola
Fe. Fi. Do.
G.
Vc.
Cb.
Fiordiligi
Dorabella
Fiordiligi
men, um eu-er Mit-leid! Him-mel, wie kühn! Ach, Schwe-ster, sag, was tun wir? Ihr Ver-
de in fle-bil me-tro! Stel-le che ar-dir! So-rel-la che fac-cia-mo? Te-me-
men, um eu-er Mit-leid!
de in fle-bil me-tro!
45
Fi.
[Despina geht erschreckt ab]
[Despina sorte impaurita]
weg-nen, ent-fer-net schnell euch aus un-srer Nä-he: Entweiht nicht län-ger durch gift'-gen Hauch der fre-vel-haf-ten
ra-ri, sor-ti-te fuo-ri di que-sto lo-co: e non pro-fa-ni l'a-li-to in-fau-sto degl'in-fa-mi
48
Re-de un-ser Herz, un-sre Oh-ren und un-sre Sin-ne! Es ist um-sonst, was ihr ver-
det-ti no-stro cor, no-stro o-rec-chio, e no-stri af-fet-ti! In-van per voi, per gli al-tri in-
f
p
cresc.
fp

Text under the vocal lines:

sucht, und nie-mals fin-det hier ihr Ge-hör,   denn heil'-ge Treu-e
van si cer-ca le no-stre al-me se-dur,   *l'in-tat-ta fe-de*

ha-ben wir schon ge-schworen,   wir sind Ver- lob-te,   und wir wah-ren die Treu
che per noi già si die-de   *ai ca-ri a-man-ti*   *sa-prem lo-ro ser-bar*

fest bis zum To- de,   wir ver-ach-ten das Le-ben,   tro-tzen dem Schicksal.
in-fi-no a mor-te,   *a dis-pet-to del mon-do*   *e del-la sor-te.*

attacca l'Aria di Fiordiligi N.º 14

№ 14. Aria

Wie der Fel-sen, der oh - ne Schwanken   trotzt ___ den Wel-len, des
Co - me sco-glio im-mo - to re - sta   con - - trai ven-ti, e

144

Recitativo

segue l'Aria di Guglielmo Nº 15

№ 15. Aria

attacca il Terzetto No 16

Mozart composed the following aria for Benucci, who sang Guglielmo in the first performance of the opera. Although the text of
this aria is in the Vienna libretto, it was not performed in Vienna
but was replaced by the aria No. 15.

№ 15a. Aria

gar nichts, ist noch gar nichts ge-gen mei-ne,
nien - te, non è nien-te in mio con-fron-te,
auch Me - do-ros, des Hel - den Wunden sind ein
un Me - do-ro il___ sen pia-ga-to ver-so

Nichts, sind ein Nichts nur ge-gen sei - ne: Glühn von Lie - be mir die Wan - gen, ist wie
lui, ver-so lui per nul-la io con - to: son di fo - coi miei so - spi - ri, son di

Wien bis Ka - na - da.
en - na al Ca - na - dà.

Bei - de sind wir reich wie Krö-sus,
Siam due Cre-si per ric-chez-za,

und noch schö-ner als Nar-
due Nar-ci-si per bel-

schal-len,_____ lockt es lieb-lich wie Nach - ti - - gal-len.
so - lo_____ fac - ciam tor - to all' u - si - -gnuo-lo,

Und noch manches wir be - si - tzen,was sich nicht so sa - gen läßt, und noch manches wir be-
e qualch' al - tro ca - pi - ta - le ab-biam poi che al-cun non sa, e qualch' al - tro ca-pi-

attacca No 16

Zwölfte Szene
Ferrando. Guglielmo. Don Alfonso.

Scena XII
Ferrando. Guglielmo. Don Alfonso.

№ 16. Terzetto

Recitativo

170

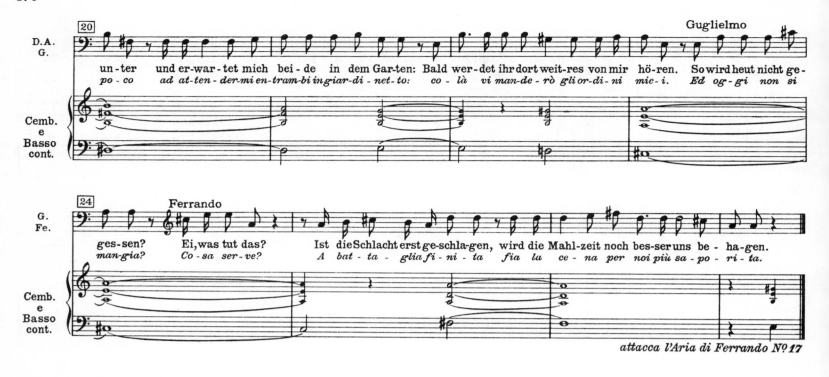

Nº 17. Aria

174

Dreizehnte Szene
Don Alfonso (allein). Dann Despina.

Scena XIII
Don Alfonso (solo), poi Despina.

Recitativo

176

segue Finale [Nº 18]

Verwandlung
Ziergärtchen. Zwei Rasenbänke an den Seiten.

Mutazione
Giardinetto gentile. Due sofa d'erba ai lati.

Vierzehnte Szene
Fiordiligi. Dorabella.

Scena XIV
Fiordiligi. Dorabella.

Nº 18. Finale

180

182

Fünfzehnte Szene

[Die Vorigen.
Ferrando, Don Alfonso und Guglielmo (hinter der Szene).
Dann Despina.]

Scena XV

[Le suddette;
Ferrando, Don Alfonso e Guglielmo (dentro le quinte),
poi Despina.]

Sechzehnte Szene

[Die Vorigen] Despina (als Arzt verkleidet). [Don Alfonso]

Scena XVI

[I suddetti.] Despina (travestita da medico). [Don Alfonso]

220

223

224

232

Ende des ersten Aktes
Fine dell' Atto primo

ZWEITER AKT
Zimmer
Erste Szene
Fiordiligi. Dorabella. Despina

ATTO SECONDO
Camera
Scena I
Fiordiligi, Dorabella e Despina.

Recitativo

segue l'Aria di Despina Nº 19

Nº 19. Aria

Wün-schen viel - leicht Sie weit-re Be - leh - rung, Ih - re De - spi - na steht zu Ge -
(Par ch'ab - bian gu - sto di tal dot - tri - na, vi - va De - spi - na che sa ser -

bot, Ih - re De - spi - na steht zu Ge - bot, Ih - re De - spi - na steht zu Ge - bot, _ steht zu Ge - bot, _ steht zu Ge - bot.
vir, vi - va De - spi - na che sa ser - vir, vi - va De - spi - na che sa ser - vir, _ che sa ser - vir, _ che sa ser - vir.)

Zweite Szene
Fiordiligi. Dorabella.

Scena II
Fiordiligi e Dorabella.

Recitativo

Duetto di Fiordiligi e Dorabella N.º 20

№ 20. Duetto

Dritte Szene
Die Vorigen. Don Alfonso.

Scena III
Le suddette e Don Alfonso.

Recitativo

Auf, geschwind in den Gar-ten, mei-ne gnä-di-gen Frau-en, wel-che Freu-de, seht Mu-si-ker und Sän-ger, ein ent-
Ah cor-re-te al giar-di-no le mie ca-re ra-gaz-ze, che al-le-gria, che mu-si-ca, che can-to, che bril-

zückendes Schauspiel, be-zaubernd! Nur geschwind und nicht zaudern! Was kann es denn nur sein? Gleich solln Sie sehen.
lan-te spet-ta-co-lo, che in-can-to! Fa-te pre-sto, cor-re-te! Che dia-mi-ne es-ser può? To-sto ve-dre-te.

[Sie gehen ab]
[Partono]

Dorabella
Don Alfonso

(Vorhang zu)

segue Duetto con Coro Nº 21

Verwandlung

Garten am Ufer des Meeres mit Rasenbänken und zwei steinernen Tischchen.
Eine blumengeschmückte Barke mit Musikanten.

Vierte Szene

Despina. Ferrando. Guglielmo. Reich gekleidete Diener.
Musikanten.
[Später Fiordiligi, Dorabella und Don Alfonso.]

Mutazione

Giardino alla riva del mare con sedili d'erba e due tavolini di pietra.
Barca ornata di fiori, con banda di stromenti.

Scena IV

Despina, Ferrando e Guglielmo. Servi riccamente vestiti.
Coro di musici.
[Poi Fiordiligi, Dorabella e Don Alfonso.]

№ 21. Duetto con Coro*)

*Lacking in the autograph MS; taken here from the MS in the Istituto Musicale, Florence.

Recitativo

segue Quartetto N.º 22

Nº 22. Quartetto

Fl.

Fag.

Tr. in D

Viol. I

Viol. II

Viola

De.

frei.   Wollt Ihr den Arm mir rei - chen: Das Seuf-zen sei vor - bei, _____ das Seuf - zen
tù.   A   me por-ge-te il brac - cio: nè so-spi-ra - te più, _____ nè so - spi -

Vc.

Cb.

sei _ vor - bei,   das Seuf - zen   sei ____ vor - bei.
ra - te _ più,   nè _ so - spi - ra - te più.

(Beiseite)
(A parte)
sotto voce

Wir ei - len schnell von
Per ca - ri - tà par -

Don Alfonso (beiseite)
(a parte)
sotto voce

Wir ei - len schnell von
Per ca - ri - tà par -

278

Fünfte Szene

[Guglielmo am Arme Dorabellas.
Ferrando und Fiordiligi (ohne sich den Arm zu geben).]

[Kurze stumme Szene, in der sie sich anschauen, seufzen und lächeln]

Scena V

[Guglielmo al braccio di Dorabella.
Ferrando e Fiordiligi (senza darsi braccio)]

[Fanno una piccola scena muta guardandosi, sospirando, ridendo]

Recitativo

No 23. Duetto

77
Clar. in C
Fag.
Cor. in F
Viol. I II
Viola
Do.
Welch Glück oh - ne - glei - chen,
Oh cam - bio fe - li - ce
G.
fällt dir der Tausch? Welch Glück oh - ne - glei - chen,
me - glio può an - dar. Oh cam - bio fe - li - ce
Vc.
Cb.
84
die Her - zen zu tau - schen, in Lieb uns be - rau - schen, in Won - ne ver - gehn, in
di co - ri e d'af - fet - ti, che nuo - vi di - let - ti, che dol - ce pe - nar, che

N.B.: Usually there is a cut between this point and the recitative on p. 312.

*Often omitted, together with the aria that follows.

290

segue l'Aria di Ferrando [Nr. 24]

*According to an indication by Mozart in the autograph MS, the following aria should be omitted and the recitative on p. 300 should follow at once.

Nr. 24. Aria

Siebente Szene
Fiordiligi (allein).

Scena VII
Fiordiligi (sola).

Recitativo *)

*Lacking in the autograph MS; taken here from the MS in the Istituto Musicale, Florence.

segue Rondo [N° 25]

№ 25. Rondo

*In the autograph MS, g#¹.

*In the autograph MS, *g#*¹.

309

Achte Szene
Ferrando. Guglielmo.

Scena VIII
Ferrando, Guglielmo.

Recitativo

attacca l'Aria di Guglielmo № 26

Nr. 26. Aria

318

sel-ber, tau-send-mal zog ich den De-gen, eu - ret - we-gen, von Na - tur seid ihr so schön
mostro, mil - le vol-te il bran-do pre-si, vi di - fe - si, gran te - so - ri il ciel vi diè,

bis zu den Zehn, doch... doch... doch... das ihr's so treibt mit al - len, mit
si - no ai piè, ma... ma... ma... la fa - te a tan - ti e tan - ti, a

162
Fl.
Ob.
Fag.
Cor. in G
Viol. I
Viol. II
Viola
G.
Vc.
Cb.
a 2
cresc.
[p]
ha-ben sie auch recht, da ha - ben sie auch recht, ganz recht, ja, da ha-ben sie auch
cer-to un gran per - chè, un gran per - che, un gran per - chè, han - no cer-to un gran per -
170
[f]
[Geht ab]
[Parte]
recht.
chè.

Neunte Szene

Ferrando (allein). Dann Don Alfonso und Guglielmo
(die sich im Hintergrund halten).

Scena IX

Ferrando (solo); poi Don Alfonso e Guglielmo
(che parlano in fondo).

Recitativo*)

*Often omitted, together with the following cavatina.

segue la Cavatina di Ferrando Nº 27

№ 27. Cavatina*)

Recitativo

Verwandlung
[Ein Zimmer mit mehreren Türen, ein Spiegel und ein Tischchen.]

Zehnte Szene
Dorabella. Despina. Dann Fiordiligi.

Mutazione
[Camera con diverse porte, specchio e tavolino.]

Scena X
Dorabella, Despina e poi Fiordiligi.

Recitativo

36 Despina: Jetzt er-kenn ich Sie wie-der als er-fah-re-ne Da-me. Dorabella: Um-sonst, De-spi-na, woll-te ich wi-der-
O - ra ve - do che sie - te u - na don - na di gar - bo. In - van De - spi - na, di re - si - ster ten -

(Vorhang auf)

39 Do.: stehn: Der klei-ne Teu-fels-kerl ist be-zau-bernd, ist so be-red-sam, so ar-tig, daß kein Fel-sen auf Er-den wi-der-
tai: quel de-mo-niet-to haun ar-ti-fi-zio, un' e-lo-quen-za, un trat-to, che ti fà ca-der giù se sei di

42 Despina: stehn kann. Schockschwerenot, zum Teu-fel, das nenn ich klug ge-spro-chen, nur zu sel-ten gibt's für uns ar-me Mäd-chen was
sas-so. Cor-po di sa-ta-nas-so, que-sto vuol dir sa-per, tan-to di ra-ro noi po-ve-re ra-gaz-ze ab-

46 De.: Gu-tes zu er-ha-schen, drum ist's klug, die Ge-le-gen-heit beim Schopf zu fas-sen. Doch sehn Sie Ih-re Schwester, was
bia-moun po di be-ne, che bi-so-gna pi-gliar-lo al-lor ch'ei vie-ne. Ma ec-co la so-rel-la, che

50 Fiordiligi: ist ihr! Un-glück-sel'-ge, Him-mel, in wel-che La-ge bin ich durch eu-re Schuld ge-kom-men! Despina: Was ge-
cef-fo! Scia-gu-ra-te, ec-co per col-pa vo-stra in che sta-to mi tro-vo! Co-sa è

53 Dorabella: schah denn, gnä-di-ges, teu-res Fräu-lein? Fiordiligi: Was hast du denn, o Schwe-ster? Ich wollt, der Teu-fel hol-te mich,
na-to, ca-ra Ma-da-mi-gel-la? Hai qual-che mal so-rel-la? Ho il dia-vo-lo, che por-ti me,

*The following bars are supplied from the MS in the Landesbibliothek, Dresden; for the version in the autograph MS, see Supplement I, p. 433.

Nº 28. Aria

Ein lo - ser Dieb ist A - mor, ein Schlänglein vol - ler List, _ er raubt und gibt den Frie-den, den
E a - mo-re un la-dron-cel - lo, un ser - pen-tel-lo è a-mor, _ ei to - glie e dà _ la pa - ce, la

341

lo - ser Dieb ist A - mor, ein Schläng-lein vol - ler List,__ er raubt und gibt den Frie-den, den Frie-den,
mo-re un la - dron-cel - lo, un ser - pen-tel-lo è a - mor,__ ei to - glie e dà__ la pa - ce, la pa - ce

wie's ihm ge-fäl - lig ist.
co - me gli pia-ce ai cor.

Er schen-ket Won-ne den sel' - gen Her-zen, läßt du ihn ru-hig
Por - ta__ dol - cez - za, dol-cez - za e gu - sto se tu lo la-sci

347

Elfte Szene

Fiordiligi (allein).
Dann Ferrando, Don Alfonso und Guglielmo
(die, ungesehen von ihr, vorbeigehen). Später Despina.

Scena XI

Fiordiligi (sola);
poi Ferrando, Don Alfonso e Guglielmo
(che passano senza esser veduti), indi Despina

Recitativo *)

Fiordiligi:
Al-les hat sich verschworen, mein Herz zu ver-füh-ren, doch nein... eher sterben als mich er-ge-ben... Ich fehl-te, als ich der
Co-me tut-to con-giu-ra a se-dur-re il mio cor, ma no... si mo-ra, e non si ce-da... er-rai quan-do al-la

Schwester und De-spi-na mein Füh-len gleich ent-deck-te. Sie er-zäh-len ihm al-les, er wird noch küh-ner, wird zum Äu-ßer-sten
suo-ra io mi sco-per-si, ed al-la ser-va mi-a. Es-se a lui di-ran tut-to, ed ei più au-da-ce fia di tut-to ca-

fä-hig... nie soll er wie-der mir vor die Au-gen kom-men... all mei-ne Leu-te be-droh ich mit Ent-
pa-ce... a-gli oc-chi mie-i mai più non com-pa-ri-sca... a tut-ti i ser-vi mi-nac-cie-rò il con-

[Guglielmo wird mit den beiden an der Tür sichtbar]
[Guglielmo sulla porta]

Guglielmo

las-sung, öff-nen sie ihm die Tür... die-sen Ver-füh-rer will ich nicht mehr sehn. (Bra-vis-si-ma, mei-ne
ge-do se lo la-scian pas-sar... ve-der nol vo-glio quel se-dut-tor. (Bra-vis-si-ma, la mia

Fiordiligi

keu-sche Ar-te-mis, hört ihr's al-le?) Doch es könnt Do-ra-bel-la, oh-ne daß ich es wüß-te...
ca-sta Ar-te-mi-sia, la sen-ti-te?) Ma po-tria Do-ra-bel-la sen-za sa-pu-ta mi-a...

halt... ein Ge-dan-ke fährt mir plötz-lich durch den Sinn... in un-serm Hau-se sind ein Paar U-ni-for-men
pia-no... un pen-sie-ro per la men-te mi pas-sa... in ca-sa mi-a re-star mol-ti u-ni-for-mi

*The following recitative is from the MS in the Istituto Musicale, Florence; for the version in the autograph MS, written in a hand other than Mozart's,
see Supplement II, p. 433.

Zwölfte Szene

[Fiordiligi. Dann Ferrando.
Später Don Alfonso und Guglielmo (an der Tür).]

Scena XII

[Fiordiligi, poi Ferrando,
indi Don Alfonso e Guglielmo (dalla porta).]

segue Duetto [N⁰ 29]

№ 29. Duetto

357

Dreizehnte Szene

Don Alfonso. Guglielmo. Dann Ferrando.

Scena XIII

Don Alfonso, Guglielmo, poi Ferrando.

Recitativo*⁾

Guglielmo

Ach, ich be-trog-ner Mann, was mußt ich se-hen, ach, und was mußt ich hö-ren! Um Got-tes wil-len,
Ah po-ve-ret-to me, co-sa ho ve-du-to, co-sa ho sen-ti-to ma-i. Per ca-ri-tà, si-

Don Alfonso

Guglielmo

ru-hig! Den Bart möcht ich zer-rau-fen, die Haut mir zer-flei-schen, an der Mau-er die Stir-ne zer-
len-zio! Mi pe-le-rei la bar-ba, mi graf-fie-rei la pel-le, e da-rei col-le cor-na en-tro le

schmet-tern, war das mei-ne Fior-di-li-gi, die Pe-ne-lo-pe und die Ar-te-mis ih-res Sä-ku-lums, die
stel-le, fu quel-la Fior-di-li-gi, la Pe-ne-lo-pe, l'Ar-te-mi-sia del se-co-lo, bric-

*The following recitative and the Andante No. 30 are lacking in the autograph MS; taken here from a MS in the Istituto Musicale, Florence.

[segue Andante Nº 30]

Vierzehnte Szene
Die Vorigen. Despina.

Recitativo

Scena XIV
I suddetti e Despina.

segue Finale [Nº 31]

Verwandlung

[Äußerst festlich erleuchteter Saal. Im Hintergrund ein Orchester.
Eine Tafel für vier Personen mit Silberleuchtern.
Vier reichgekleidete Diener.]

Fünfzehnte Szene

Despina. Chor der Diener und Musikanten.
Dann Don Alfonso

Mutazione

[Sala ricchissima illuminata. Orchestra in fondo.
Tavola per quattro persone con doppieri d'argento.
Quattro servi riccamente vestiti.]

Scena XV

Despina. Coro di Servi e di Suonatori,
poi Don Alfonso.

№ 31. Finale

369

Sechzehnte Szene

[Die Vorigen. Fiordiligi. Dorabella. Ferrando. Guglielmo.]

[Während sie nach vorn kommen, singt der Chor und das Orchester stimmt einen Marsch an]

Scena XVI

[I suddetti, Fiordiligi, Dorabella, Ferrando e Guglielmo.]

[Mentre s'avanzano il coro canta e incomincia l'orchestra una marcia]

Glück und Heil den bei-den ed-len Herrn und den lie-bens-wer-ten Bräu-ten, Glück und Heil den bei-den ed-len Herrn:
Be - ne - det-ti i dop-pi con-ju - gi, e le a-ma-bi-li spo-si - ne, be - ne-det-ti i dop-pi con-ju - gi:

Glück und Heil den bei-den ed-len Herrn,
Be - ne - det-ti i dop-pi con-ju - gi,

Glück und Heil den bei-den ed-len Herrn und den
be - ne-det-ti i dop-pi con-ju - gi, e le a-

378

386

388

Siebenzehnte Szene

[Die Vorigen. Don Alfonso. Dann Despina (als Notar).]

Scena XVII

[I suddetti, Don Alfonso, poi Despina (da Notajo).]

392

394

[Die Verträge bleiben in der Hand Don Alfonsos]
[La carta resta in man di Don Alfonso]

(Man hört Trommelwirbel [und Gesang hinter der Szene])
(Si sente gran suono di tamburo [e canto])

O, wie schön, Soldat zu sein, o, wie schön, Soldat zu sein! Ein Sol-dat hat nie zu sorgen, darbt er
Bel-la vi-ta mi-li-tar; bel-la vi-ta mi-li-tar! O-gni dì si cangia lo-co, og-gi

Tausend quä-len-de Ge-danken ja-gen durch den Kopf mit Schrecken, wenn sie den Ver-
Mil-le bar-ba-ri pen-sie-ri tor-men-tan-do il cor mi van-no, se dis-co-pro-

schon.

rat ent-de-cken, ach, was fan-gen wir dann an, ach, was fan-gen wir dann an!
no l'in-gan-no, ah di noi che mai sa-rà, ah di noi che mai sa-rà!

Letzte Szene

[Fiordiligi. Dorabella.
Ferrando und Guglielmo (in Uniformmänteln und Hüten).
Despina (im Nebenzimmer). Don Alfonso.]

Scena ultima

[Fiordiligi, Dorabella,
Ferrando e Guglielmo (con mantelli e cappelli militari),
Despina (in camera) e Don Alfonso.]

411

422

426

432

Ende der Oper
Fine dell' Opera

SUPPLEMENT

I

Autograph MS Ending of the Recitative, p. 339

In the autograph MS the recitative ends with the following bars. Presumably Mozart had originally intended to compose Dorabella's aria (No. 28) in a different key, or had another insertion in mind.

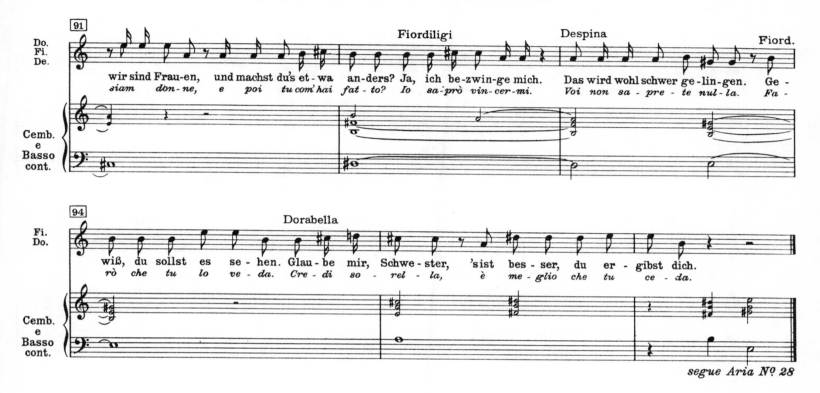

segue Aria Nº 28

II

Second Version of the Recitative, p. 348

In the autograph MS, written in a hand not Mozart's, is the following version of the same text. It cannot be assumed that this variant is by Mozart himself.

Zwölfte Szene

Fiordiligi. Dann Ferrando.
Später Guglielmo und Don Alfonso (an der Tür).

Scena XII

Fiordiligi, poi Ferrando,
indi Guglielmo e Don Alfonso (dalla porta).

[50] Fiordiligi

Hier die-ser Rock Fer-ran-dos paßt vor-treff-lich für mich, und Do-ra-bel-la nimmt hier den von Gu-
L'a - bi - to di Fer-ran-do sa - rà buo-no per me; può Do - ra - bel - la pren-der quel di Gu-

[53]

gliel-mo; in die-sen Klei-dern ge-hen wir schnell zu un-sern Freun-den, an ih-rer Sei-te wolln wir käm-pfen, und wenn's
gliel-mo; in que-sti ar-ne - si rag-giun-ge-rem gli spo-si no-stri, al lo-ro fian-co pugnar po-tre-mo, e mo-

[56] [Reißt ihren Kopfputz herunter]
[Si cava quello che tiene in testa]

sein muß, auch ster-ben: Aus mei-nen Au-gen, du un-se-li-ger Haar-schmuck... den ich ver-ach-te.
rir se fa d'uo-po: i - te in ma - lo - ra or-na-men-ti fa - ta - li... io vi de-te-sto.

[59] Guglielmo   **Fiordiligi**

(Sah man je sol-che Lie-be, sol-che Treu-e?) Hof-fe nicht, mei-ne Stirn je wie-der zu schmü-cken, bis ich mit
(Si può dar un a - mor si-mi-le a que-sto?) Di tor-nar non spe-ra-te al-la mia fron-te pria ch'io qui

[62]

ihm wie-der ver-eint: An dei-ner Stel-le will die-sen Hut ich tra-gen... ach, wie er mich ver-än-dert, mei-ne
tor-ni col mio ben: in vo-stro lo-co por-rò que-sto cap-pel-lo... oh co-me ei mi tras-for-ma le sem-

[65]

Au-gen, die Zü-ge, ja, wahr-haf-tig, ich ken-ne mich selbst kaum wie-der!
bian-ze e il vi-so, co-me ap-pe-na io me-des-ma or mi ra-vi-so!

[segue Duetto Nº 29]

Basis of the Edition

The present score is based on Mozart's own manuscript, in the collection of the Prussian State Library in Berlin. Unfortunately this manuscript is not preserved in its entirety; it lacks the duet with chorus No. 21 and the recitative "Ei parte" before the rondo No. 25. The recitative "Come congiura" before the duet No. 29 appears in the MS only in another hand, while the recitative "Ah poveretto me," together with the following Andante No. 30, is again totally missing. For the editing of these numbers it was possible to use a copy in the Istituto Musicale in Florence (Archive Pitti A.260).

Mozart evidently wrote the score in haste, often without enough time to write out all the details, using instead more abbreviations than usually occur in his MSS. In some passages this goes so far that he wrote "colla parte" for Violin I when it is in unison with the vocal part. Naturally, in such places the bowing is missing and must be supplied.

Unfortunately the MS also lacks some wind, brass and drum parts: in the sextet No. 13, the trumpets and drums; in the finale No. 18, from bar 62 on, all winds, brass and drums; and in the finale No. 31, from bar 310 on, likewise all winds, brass and drums. Mozart was unable to fit these onto the 12-staff music paper he used, and wrote them on additional sheets that seem to be irretrievably lost. For the trumpets and drums in the sextet No. 13, the MS does not refer to an additional sheet ("Extra-Blatt"), as is the usual case in all Mozart autograph MSS; but since they are found in the copies, there can be little doubt that Mozart himself later added them. For the editing of all the missing wind, brass and drum parts, we used a copy in the Sächsische Landesbibliothek in Dresden (3972 F 99) which contains them, although often in a not very reliable form.

Also consulted was a copy in the Prussian State Library in Berlin (Mus. ms. 15153/1), which helped settle many problems.

Although the autograph MS is written very clearly, there are still many slips of the pen and small oversights of the type commonly made when writing down music. Most of these errors leave no doubt about the correct readings and have been tacitly corrected. Where this was not possible and no comparison with similar passages could be made, the obviously correct versions have been incorporated into the text; whereas all other deviations from the autograph, the correctness of which was not sufficiently established, have been listed without exception in the following Editors' Commentary in order to present as faithful a picture as possible of Mozart's manuscript.

For the Italian text and the stage directions we used the printed libretto of 1790, a copy of which is in the Vienna Municipal Library (23 482). Mozart wrote Italian very accurately; here for the first time his punctuation, which makes rich and varied use of semicolons, colons and dashes, has been faithfully followed. Only in the arias and ensembles does Mozart become less careful, and for these the punctuation has been altered or supplied on the basis of the libretto. When, as it sometimes happens, the text in the autograph differs from that in the printed libretto, the version of the autograph has been considered as authoritative, and changes have been made correspondingly.

Mozart transferred Da Ponte's stage directions to the autograph only partially; on the other hand, in many places he added stage directions himself or changed some. All missing stage directions necessary for actual production have been supplied from the libretto, but placed in square brackets to show their origin clearly.

Slurs, ties and staccato marks missing in the autograph have been supplied tacitly when analogous passages or the notation of the other instruments proved them to be necessary.

Mozart's autograph contains dots, short heavy dashes and long thin dashes. In Mozart, however, the short heavy dash is not a staccato mark in our modern sense, but an accent, a "ben marcato." At any rate, in the autograph the difference between dots and dashes is not firm; many long dashes occur in places where there is no doubt, or else it is highly probable, that they signify accents, whereas certain dots are abbreviated dashes (in general Mozart scarcely seems to make a basic distinction between dots and weak dashes). However, in order to rule out any doubts, the autograph has been scrupulously followed here, insofar as possible, since the pen is more sensitive than the engraving tool.

Editors' Commentary

Ouvertura

Meas. 1 ff.: The trumpets are called "clarini" in the MS.

M. 3: Oboe I has no slur in the MS (also in mm. 6/7).

Mm. 12–14: The ties for the 2nd winds are given in the MS only for Flute II.

M. 18: In the MS, Violin I lacks staccato dots (also in m. 22).

M. 46: In the MS, Violin II lacks staccato dots. In the MS, the Basses have staccato marks on the 3rd and 4th quarters.

M. 53: In contrast to m. 189, the MS shows the *forte* in the Violins and Violas on the 1st quarter.

M. 58: In the MS, Flute I and Oboe I have no slur to the next bar.

M. 60: In the MS, Flute II and Oboe II have no tie to the next bar (also, Flute II in m. 62).

M. 65: In the MS, Bassoons and Basses have staccato marks on the 4th quarter and in the next bar.

M. 70: In the MS, Flute II has d^3 and Clarinet II has d^2; changed here to b^2 and b^1, respectively, because of the parallel octaves.

M. 71: In the MS, Oboe I lacks the slur.

Mm. 76/77: The staccato dots in the Bassoons and strings are supplied on the basis of the preceding bars.

M. 103: In the MS, the Trumpets have a tie from the 4th quarter to the next bar (also in bar 121).

M. 108: In the MS, Violin II lacks the slur to the next bar.

Mm. 110/111: In the MS, Flutes and Violin I have one slur per bar (also Oboes and Violas in mm. 126/127 and Oboes in mm. 128/129).

M. 145: In the MS, Clarinet II lacks the slur to the next bar.

Mm. 170–172: Violin I has staccato marks in the MS.

Mm. 217/218: In the MS, Trumpet II lacks the tie. The slurs in Oboe II and Clarinet II are supplied from Flute II.

M. 219: In the MS, Trumpet II has e^1 on the 1st quarter, but apparently c^1 was intended.

Mm. 233/234: In the MS, Oboe II lacks the tie.

M. 239: In the MS, Flute II, Oboe I and Clarinet I have a slur to the next bar.

M. 251: In the MS, the *forte* in Viola and Basses is not here but in the next bar.

M. 257: In the MS, the Oboes have e^2 and c^1 on the 1st quarter, apparently in confusion with the Clarinets.

No. 1. Terzetto

M. 2: In the MS, Violin I lacks the staccato marks here and in several other passages.

M. 21: In the MS, the Violas lack the staccato dots on the 4th quarter.

Mm. 47/48: In the MS, the winds lack a few slurs.

M. 50: The Bassoon I slur is supplied from Oboe I.

M. 55: In the MS, the Bassoons lack the slur.

No. 2. Terzetto

M. 12: In the MS, the Basses lack the tie to the next bar.

Mm. 35 ff.: In the MS, the string slurs are partially one bar long, partially two bars long.

M. 48: In the MS, the Violas lack the tie to the next bar (see m. 12).

No. 3. Terzetto

M. 11: The staccato marks in Viola I are supplied.

M. 15: In the MS, Violin I has only one slur, here changed to two on the basis of m. 13.

M. 23: Some string staccato marks on the 3rd and 4th quarters are supplied (also in m. 27).

M. 31: The Bassoon slurs, missing in the MS, are supplied from the Oboe part.

Mm. 34/35: The Bassoon staccato dots, missing in the MS, are supplied from the Viola part.

Mm. 38/39: The staccato dots in Bassoons and Cellos are supplied; in m. 39, in the Violas as well (also in mm. 63/64 in Bassoons, Violas and Basses).

M. 43: In the MS, the winds, Drum, Violas and Basses have *forte* again on the 1st quarter.

Mm. 44/45: In the Violas and Basses, the staccato marks on the 2nd and 3rd quarters are supplied.

Mm. 49/50: The Trumpets lack the slur in the MS.

No. 4. Duetto

M. 1: The Bassoon staccato mark (m. 3 in Clarinets and Bassoons) is supplied.

M. 6: In the MS, the Violin I grace note is notated as a 32nd note (also in mm. 8, 19 and 21).

M. 7: In the MS, Violin II and Violas have another *piano*.

M. 21: In the MS, the Basses have *forte* instead of *mezzo forte*.

M. 27: In the MS, the Violas lack the slur.

Mm. 35/36: In the MS, the Violin I staccato marks are indicated only on the 1st quarter of m. 35.

Mm. 51/52: In the MS, Violin II lacks the slurs.

M. 62: In the MS, the Violas lack the slur to the next bar.

Mm. 66/67: In the MS, Viola II lacks the tie.

Mm. 78/79: In the MS, the Violas lack the slurs.

Mm. 104–107: The MS shows the staccato marks only for the Basses.

M. 131: The Violin I/II staccato mark is supplied from the Viola part.

M. 152: The MS lacks the staccato dots on the 2nd quarter in Violin II.

No. 5. Aria

Mm. 4 ff.: In some places the MS lacks the staccato marks for Violin I/II.

Mm. 12/13: In the MS, here and in mm. 33–36 the Viola lacks the slurs; also in Viola II, mm. 30–32.

No. 6. Quintetto

Mm. 34/35: The Bassoon I slurs, missing in the MS, are supplied from the Clarinet part.

Mm. 39/40: The Clarinet and Bassoon slur, missing in the MS, is supplied from mm. 68/69.

M. 57: The slurs in Clarinet I and Bassoon I are missing in the MS (also in m. 86).

Mm. 61/62: The Viola slur is supplied from the Bass part.

M. 63: The Bass slur is supplied from m. 92.

M.	68:	In the MS, Violins I/II here, in contrast to m. 39, have two slurs, one on quarters 1–3 and one on the 4th.
M.	69:	In the MS, in contrast to m. 40, Fiordiligi has two quarter notes.
M.	77:	The grace notes for Fiordiligi and Dorabella are lacking in the MS, but are indicated in m. 48.
M.	99:	In the MS, the Violas have merely *forte* (also in m. 101).
M.	107:	In the MS, Oboe II has another *piano*. The MS lacks the Bassoon slurs.

No. 7. Duettino

M.	3:	The MS lacks the Viola and Bass staccato marks.

No. 8. Coro

M.	24:	The MS lacks the staccato mark in this bar.
M.	25:	From the 4th quarter through m. 39, and from m. 42 to the end, the wind and Drum parts are not written out in the MS, but merely indicated by "Come prima" (Flute and Oboe are written out from m. 49, 4th quarter, to m. 50).

Recitativo

M.	12:	In the MS, "Segue coi stromenti," since the next number is labeled not as a quintet, but as a recitative (and so the key is not indicated).

No. 9. Quintetto

M.	14:	In the MS, the Violas have the *forte* on the 3rd quarter.
M.	17:	The MS lacks the Viola slur (also in m. 21).
M.	18:	The Bassoon II slur is supplied from m. 22.
M.	19:	The Bassoon I slur is supplied.
M.	27:	In the MS: "attacca il Coro No. 8 qui si ripete il Coro (bella vita militar)."

No. 10. Terzettino

M.	8:	The first Clarinet I slur is supplied (also in m. 10).
M.	10:	The Bassoon slur is supplied from m. 8.
M.	13:	The Clarinet I slur is supplied.
M.	13–15:	The Clarinet II slurs are supplied (also in m. 16).
M.	31:	The MS lacks the Clarinet slur.
M.	37:	In the MS, the Violin I/II *forte* does not appear until the 3rd quarter.
M.	38:	From the 3rd quarter on, the MS erroneously notates the Clarinets a tone too low.
M.	40:	The MS lacks the Violin I slur.

Recitativo

Mm.	16/17:	The MS lacks the Viola staccato dots.
Mm.	19/20:	In the MS, the Basses have a slur over both bars.
M.	22:	The Violin II staccato dots are supplied.
Mm.	22–24:	The MS notates the Violin I grace notes as 16th notes.
M.	24:	In the MS, the Bass *forte* appears on the 1st quarter.

No. 11. Aria

M.	17:	The MS lacks the Clarinet II tie.
Mm.	20/21:	In the MS, Flute I has another slur from the 1st to the 2nd halfnote (also in mm. 60/61).
M.	49:	In the MS, the Bassoons have only *mezzo forte* (also in m. 51).
M.	87:	The Bassoon slur is supplied from m. 79.
Mm.	94/95:	The Clarinet II slur is supplied from the Flute II part.
Mm.	95/96:	The Clarinet I tie is supplied from the Flute I part.

No. 12. Aria

M.	10:	The MS lacks the Violin I staccato marks.
M.	19:	In the MS, Oboe, Violin I and Bass lack the slur to the next bar.
M.	27:	In the MS, the Violin I slur ends on the 1st eighth note, and the next one begins immediately on the 2nd eighth note.
Mm.	43/44:	The Oboe and Bassoon slurs are altered to match all the others. The MS lacks the Violin II tie.
Mm.	61/62:	In the MS, the slurs are written very hastily and irregularly (also in mm. 87/88).
M.	64:	The Violin I/II staccato dots are supplied (also in mm. 77/78).
M.	69:	The Flute trill mark is lacking in the MS (also in M. 77).
M.	86:	The MS gives the *forte* in various places, altered here on the basis of the Bassoon and Violin I parts. The Viola markings are supplied from m. 84.

No. 13. Sestetto

Mm.	1 ff.:	The MS lacks the Trumpet and Drum parts, edited here from the Dresden copy.
M.	12:	The MS lacks the Bassoon slur.
M.	14:	The Violin II slurs are supplied.
Mm.	15–21:	The Bassoon slurs, partly missing, are supplied from the Clarinet and Violin parts.
M.	20:	The MS lacks the Violin I/II slur.
M.	31:	In the Dresden copy, the Trumpet lacks the tie to the next bar.
M.	43:	The MS gives the *forte* in various places.
Mm.	44/45:	The MS shows the staccato marks only in the winds, and also in Violin I/II, m. 44, 3rd and 4th quarters.
M.	48:	The MS lacks the Oboe II tie to the next bar.
M.	51:	The MS lacks the Bass staccato dots (which are supplied throughout in mm. 52/53).
M.	54:	The MS lacks the Bass staccato dots here and in m. 58 (they are supplied throughout in mm. 55 and 59).
M.	56:	The MS lacks the Oboe slur (also in m. 60).
M.	70–72:	The MS gives the staccato marks only for Violin I/II in m. 72; all the rest are supplied.
M.	90:	The MS lacks the Bassoon II slur.
M.	102:	The MS lacks the Clarinet and Bassoon I slur (also Oboe II and Bassoon II, m. 112).
M.	152:	The Dresden copy lacks the Trumpet ties to the next bar, but indicates them in m. 196.
M.	195:	In the MS, Bassoons and Basses have another *forte* here.
M.	198:	The MS lacks the staccato dots on the 3rd and 4th quarters, but gives them in m. 154.

No. 14. Aria

M.	9:	The MS gives the staccato mark here only in the Basses, and also adds another *piano* there.
M.	24:	In the MS, Violin II has *e*¹ on the 4th quarter; changed here to *g*¹ on the basis of m. 26.
M.	32:	The MS lacks the Violin I staccato marks (also in Violas and Basses, m. 37).
Mm.	79–81:	The Oboe and Clarinet staccato dots are supplied (also in mm. 84–86).
M.	89:	The Violin I staccato dots on the 4th quarter are supplied (as are all the dots for Violin II, m. 90).
M.	101:	The MS shows the staccato marks only in the Basses.
Mm.	117–120:	The Bass staccato marks are supplied.
M.	124:	In the MS, Bassoon II has another slur.

No. 15. Aria

M.	37:	The MS lacks the Violin II slur.
M.	38:	The MS lacks the Violin I/II staccato mark.

No. 15a. Aria

M. 34: The MS begins the wind slur in the next bar; changed here on the basis of m. 40.
Mm. 64/65: The MS lacks the Oboe I slur.
M. 84: The MS distributes the *forte* unevenly among the strings; changed here on the basis of Violin I.
Mm. 96–106: The Violin II and Viola staccato dots are supplied.
M. 114: The MS gives Guglielmo *g-a* instead of *a-b* on the last eighth.
M. 155: The MS has only *forte* in Bassoon, Viola and Bass.
M. 167: The MS lacks the Violin I/II staccato mark (in m. 169, the winds and Violin I/II have the slur up to the 3rd quarter, and also lack the staccato mark).
M. 189: The MS lacks the Violin II staccato dots (in m. 193 they are also missing in Violin I on the 3rd and 4th quarters).
M. 194: The MS lacks the Violin II tie to the next bar.

No. 16. Terzetto

M. 3: The MS already has "Sempre stacc." on m. 1.
M. 17: In the MS, Oboes and Violin I/II do not have the *forte* until the 3rd quarter. In the MS, Oboe I has a slur from the 1st to the 3rd quarter.
M. 21: The MS lacks the Bassoon tie to the next bar (also in m. 53).
M. 31: The MS lacks the Oboe slur.
M. 59: In the MS, the Basses do not have the *forte* until the next bar.

No. 17. Aria

M. 15: The MS gives the staccato mark only in the Basses (also in m. 55).
M. 22: The MS lacks the Violin II slur.
M. 53: The staccato marks, except for the one on the 2nd eighth note of Violin I, are supplied from m. 13.
M. 57: The MS lacks the Bassoon I tie to the next bar.
Mm. 60/61: The Bass slur is supplied from mm. 20/21.
M. 61: The Clarinet II and Bassoon I/II slurs are supplied.
Mm. 71/72: The Bassoon slurs are supplied.

Recitativo

Here and in a few other places in the stage directions Mozart wrote "Despinetta."

No. 18. Finale

M. 12: The MS lacks the Horn staccato dots on the 2nd quarter and the next bar.
M. 19: The Violin I slur here and in m. 50 is supplied from m. 2.
M. 31: The MS lacks the Bass staccato marks.
M. 47: The MS lacks the Bassoon slur.
M. 48: In the MS, the Flute has merely *forte piano*.
Mm. 62 ff.: The MS lacks the Oboe and Trumpet parts: "NB. Oboe, Clarini sono scritti a parte"; unfortunately the separate leaf is lost. The Flute and Bassoon parts are entered in a different hand; the indication "extra blatt" is crossed out; from m. 97 on, Flute and Bassoon are missing altogether. All wind parts are edited from the Dresden copy.
M. 67: In the MS, Violin I/II have more staccato marks— on the 2nd–4th eighth notes.
M. 72: The Viola and Bass staccato marks are supplied, as are all of them in the next two bars.
M. 77: The MS lacks the Bassoon slur; in the next bar, a slur is drawn in from the 1st to the 2nd note, but this does not occur for any other instrument.
M. 78: In the MS, Bassoons and Horns [Trumpets?] have *forte piano*, Violas and Basses only *forte*.
M. 79: The MS lacks the Flute slur, the Oboe slurs on the 3rd and 4th quarters, and all those for the Bassoons.
M. 88: The MS lacks the Bassoon slur (also in mm. 91 and 107).

M. 92: The Viola tie to the next bar is supplied from m. 108.
M. 93: The Violin I/II staccato mark is supplied from m. 109.
Mm. 99–102: The Bassoon part in the Dresden copy is very inexact.
M. 107: The MS divides the Violin I/II slur by half-bars.
Mm. 132/133: The MS gives the staccato marks only for Violin I, m. 132.
Mm. 138 ff.: The MS lacks all wind, brass and Drums to the end of the act; they are edited from the Dresden copy, which is very inexact in the phrasing and dynamic markings, so that many had to be supplied.
Mm. 175 ff.: Here and in a few later bars Mozart notated the string slurs by full bars.
Mm. 200–202: The Dresden copy gives Clarinet I *d¹* instead of *f¹*.
M. 207: The MS lacks the Violin I staccato dots on the 3rd and 4th quarters (also in mm. 209 and 211).
M. 211: The Dresden copy gives Clarinet II *d¹* instead of *f¹* on the 4th quarter.
M. 224: From here to m. 259, the MS lacks all string staccato dots.
Mm. 301/302: The MS gives staccato dots only in the Violas and Basses in m. 301; all others are supplied (also in mm. 305 and 307/308).
M. 316: The Dresden copy gives the Oboes *forte*.
Mm. 319 f.: In the Dresden copy the Horns have wrong dynamics (in m. 325 all winds and brass have only *piano* instead of *forte piano*).
Mm. 331/332: The MS lacks the Bass slur and staccato marks.
Mm. 333–335: All staccato marks are supplied from m. 332.
Mm. 363–365: The Bassoon part in the Dresden copy is incorrect.
Mm. 365–368: The Violin I/II and Viola staccato marks are supplied.
Mm. 377–379: All the staccato marks are supplied.
Mm. 385–390: The MS lacks wind and brass, which are on a separate enclosed sheet in a different hand, with the Clarinets apparently forgotten.
M. 392: The Viola staccato marks, and those for all the strings in m. 393, are supplied.
M. 400: In the Dresden copy the Oboe and Bassoon parts are incorrect.
M. 433: The Dresden copy lacks the *piano* on the 1st quarter of winds and brass. It is indicated for the Bassoons on the 2nd quarter, for Clarinets and Trumpets not until the next bar.
Mm. 442 ff.: The dynamic markings in smaller type are in both the Dresden and Berlin copies.
M. 446: The slur on the 4th quarter in Clarinets and Bassoons is supplied.
Mm. 483/484: The Dresden copy lacks the Horn I tie.
Mm. 485 ff.: In the MS and the copies, the Flute and Violin I dotted halfnote is partially within the slur, and partially the slur is only over the 4th quarter.
Mm. 505–511: The Bass staccato marks are supplied from mm. 576 ff. (as a result the Viola marks are supplied in both places); in mm. 513/514 and 584/585 the MS gives them only in the Basses.
Mm. 546–556: The Clarinet slurs are supplied.
Mm. 571 ff.: The orchestra is not written out in the MS, but called for by "istromenti." In mm. 586–594 Violin I is written out, in mm. 593/594 Violin II and Violas, whereas in mm. 595–627, inclusive, again only "istromenti" is indicated.
M. 588: Here and in mm. 590 and 592 the Dresden copy gives the Horns, Trumpets and Drums *forte*, and *piano* again in mm. 589, 591 and 593.
Mm. 597/598: The Dresden copy gives Trumpet II *a¹*.
M. 607: The MS gives the Basses *sf* (in m. 536 *forte*, as here).
M. 629: The copies give the Horns *forte* instead of *piano* (also in m. 643).
Mm. 631/632: Some of the Violin I/II staccato dots here and in mm. 643 ff. are supplied.
Mm. 677–680: The copies give the winds a few slurs.
Mm. 689 ff.: A few staccato dots are supplied.

No. 19. Aria

Mm. 23 ff.: Here and in a few other places Violin I is indicated by "colla parte"; therefore phrasing and dynamics had to be supplied.

M.   55: The Flute, Bassoon and Violin I staccato mark is supplied from m. 57 (also in m. 91).
M.   85: The MS gives the Flutes and Violin I/II a dotted halfnote.

No. 20. Duetto

Mm. 21–24: In the MS, two Viola slurs cover two bars each.
Mm. 71/72: The MS gives the Bassoons a slur over both bars.

No. 21. Duetto con Coro

M.   15: The Bassoon slur is supplied (also the one in Horn I, m. 16).
M.   37: The Bassoon I slur is supplied.
Mm. 37/38: All Horn slurs and ties are supplied (also for Horn I, m. 40).
Mm. 56/57: The Horn II slur is supplied.
M.   67: The slurs in Flute II, Clarinet II and Horn I are supplied (also in Horn I, m. 68).
M.   71: The Florence copy gives Clarinet II $e\flat^1$ instead of g^1.

Recitativo

M.   23: The MS has "segue Aria di Don Alfonso," although the next number has no heading at all.

No. 22. Quartetto

Mm.   1–3: The Flute staccato dots are supplied.
Mm.   3/4: The Violin II, Viola and Bass slurs are supplied, as is the one in Violas and Basses in mm. 7/8 (see mm. 45/46).
M.   7: The Violin I staccato mark is supplied (also in mm. 20 and 45).
M.   28: The MS lacks the Violin I/II staccato dots.
Mm. 43–45: Some Flute and Violin I/II staccato dots are supplied (also the Bassoon staccato mark in m. 45).
Mm. 84/85: The MS lacks the Flute II slur.

No. 23. Duetto

M.   32: The MS lacks the Bassoon I slur (also the one in Bassoon II, m. 34).
Mm. 39–41: The MS lacks the Viola staccato marks (for all the strings, m. 41); in m. 44 they are given again for Violin I.
Mm. 79–85: The MS gives the Clarinet and Bassoon slur only up to m. 83 (in mm. 95–101, only up to m. 100).
M.   91: The string staccato marks are supplied from m. 107, where they are given except for the Basses.
Mm. 109/110: The MS lacks the Bass slur.
Mm. 111/112: The Horn slurs and ties are supplied from mm. 113/114.
M.   117: The Violin I staccato dots are supplied.

Recitativo

M.   23: The MS has, in Mozart's hand: "Dopo questo viene Scena 7ma Recitativo Istromentato di Fiordiligi e Rondo 25."

No. 24. Aria

M.   8: The Bass staccato mark is supplied from m. 50.
M.   23: The MS gives Violin I/II another *piano*.
Mm. 24–26: In the MS, the Violin II slurs are divided by half-bars (later, too, in some Violin I/II passages).
Mm. 102–104: The MS lacks the staccato dots in the winds.
M.   126: The MS already gives the Clarinets the following slur on the 3rd quarter of this bar (see m. 129).

Recitativo

M.   1: The Dresden copy gives a $B\flat$ major chord on the 1st quarter, while the Berlin copy has a $B\flat$ only in the Basses; we here follow the Florence copy.

No. 25. Rondo

Mm.   1 ff.: The MS notates the Clarinets in B.
M.   11: The MS lacks the Bassoon staccato marks.
M.   38: The MS lacks the Violin I staccato marks (also in m. 68).
Mm. 54/55: The MS lacks the Bassoon slurs (also the one in m. 74).

Recitativo

M.   64: The MS gives the Basses *forte* instead of *cresc.*
Mm. 79/80: A few staccato marks are supplied.
Mm. 81/82: The MS lacks the Bass slur (also in mm. 84/85 and 95/96).
M.   85: In the MS, the Basses have an eighth note instead of a quarter.
M.   86: The Violin I staccato marks are supplied from m. 88.

No. 26. Aria

Mm.   5/6: Staccato dots are given only on the 1st quarter in the Flutes in m. 5.
Mm. 33/34: The Viola slur is supplied from the Bass part.
M.   47: The Oboe II and Bassoon I/II slurs are supplied.
Mm. 57/58: The Horn staccato dots are supplied (in mm. 112/113, too, they are given only in the Flute part).
M.   68: The MS gives only the Flute staccato dots.
M.   77: The Violin I staccato dots on the 2nd quarter and in the next bar are supplied (also in mm. 134/135).
Mm. 91/92: The Flute and Bassoon staccato dots are supplied.
M.   96: The bass tie to the next bar is not in the MS.
M.   105: The MS lacks the Violin I staccato dots (also in m. 107).
Mm. 121/122: The MS lacks the Violin II slur.
M.   131: The MS lacks the Violin II staccato dots (also Violin II, m. 133). Moreover, a few are supplied in mm. 137–141 and 145–149.
Mm. 154/155: The Bass staccato marks are supplied (as are all in m. 161).
Mm. 164–167: The MS lacks the Bassoon slurs.
Mm. 168/169: The MS lacks the Oboe slurs.

Recitativo

M.   6: In the MS, Violin I has only *sf* (also in m. 12).
M.   26: The MS gives staccato marks only in the Bass part.

No. 27. Cavatina

Mm. 11–13: The Violin I slurs are altered on the basis of mm. 41–43.
M.   36: In contrast to m. 6, the MS gives the *forte* on the 1st quarter. The MS lacks the Viola slur (see m. 6).
M.   40: The MS lacks the Horn I/II slur.
M.   44: The Viola staccato mark is supplied.
M.   57: The MS gives Oboe I another *piano*.
Mm. 59 ff.: The MS notates the Clarinets in F major (*f#* and *c#* have separate accidentals).

No. 28. Aria

M.   1: The MS lacks the Clarinet I staccato marks (also in m. 5).
M.   31: The MS gives the Oboe *forte* on the 4th eighth note.
M.   33: In contrast to the other passages, the MS here and in m. 37 notates the vocal grace notes as eighth notes. The MS gives the Horns another *piano* (also in mm. 39 and 40).

Mm.	40/41:	The MS divides the Clarinet and Bassoon slur in two by bars (change of staff in the MS).
M.	65:	The MS lacks the Oboe and Clarinet I staccato mark and 2nd slur.
M.	70:	The MS lacks the Clarinet II staccato marks (also in m. 101).
M.	72:	The Bassoon I staccato marks are supplied.
M.	83:	The MS lacks the Oboe staccato dots.
Mm.	94/95:	A few staccato dots are supplied.
M.	107:	The MS lacks the Bassoon II slur.
M.	110:	The slurs in Clarinet I and Violin I are supplied.

No. 29. Duetto

Mm.	6/7:	The Bass staccato marks are supplied.
M.	8:	The MS lacks the Viola slur.
M.	25:	The Bassoon slur is supplied (also in m. 27).
M.	30:	The MS lacks the Violin I staccato marks on the 2nd quarter (also in m. 32).
Mm.	47/48:	The MS divides the Violin II slur by bars.
M.	54:	The Bass slur is supplied (also in m. 56).
Mm.	74/75:	The MS gives the slur only in Oboe II and Bassoon I.
M.	88:	The MS gives the strings another *piano*.
Mm.	95/96:	The MS lacks the Bassoon slur and tie.
M.	114:	The Violin I staccato marks are supplied (as is the 2nd one in Violin II).
M.	132:	The MS divides the Oboe and Violin I/II slurs by half-bars.
Mm.	135/136:	The Oboe slur is supplied.

No. 30. Andante

Mm.	23–26:	These bars are mutilated in the Berlin and Florence copies; given here from the Dresden copy.

No. 31. Finale

Mm.	1 ff.:	A few missing staccato marks in Violin I are supplied.
M.	5:	The MS gives Bassoon I a slur to the next bar.
M.	46:	The MS gives the Oboes and Bassoons another *piano*.
Mm.	68/69:	The string staccato dots are supplied from mm. 72/73.
Mm.	74–76:	The Bass staccato marks are supplied.
Mm.	77–80:	The MS lacks the Clarinet II and Bassoon I/II slurs.
M.	79:	The MS lacks the Violin I staccato marks.
M.	84:	The MS lacks the wind slur on the 1st half of the bar.
M.	93:	The Clarinet II slur is supplied.
M.	96:	The MS lacks the Violin II slur on the 1st quarter.
M.	119:	The MS lacks the Clarinet I slur on the 4th quarter.
Mm.	124 ff.:	The repeat is not written out in the MS, but called for by: "Coro dal Segno 18 battute."
M.	172:	The MS lacks the Bassoon staccato marks.
M.	187:	The MS lacks the Violin II slur.
M.	198:	The MS lacks the Violin II staccato marks.
Mm.	210–214:	The Flute I and Bass slurs are supplied.
Mm.	212/213:	The Violin II staccato dots are supplied.
M.	218:	The Violin II staccato dots and those for Violin I/II in m. 219 are supplied.

M.	224:	In the MS and all copies, Violin I has ♮ instead of ♯ in front of the d^1.
Mm.	224/225:	In the MS, the Violin II and Viola slurs are divided by bars (also from m. 234 on).
Mm.	236/237:	The MS gives the Viola part incorrectly (confused with mm. 238/239).
M.	239:	The MS lacks the Oboe II tie to the next bar. The MS gives Violin I a^1 instead of $a\#^1$.
Mm.	287–289:	The MS lacks the Bassoon staccato dots (m. 289, Oboe, too).
M.	289:	The MS gives the Flutes *sf*.
Mm.	310 ff.:	From here on, winds, brass and Drums are missing in the MS. Only in the very last tempo, "Allegro molto," p. 422, is the prelude melody given for 8 bars, and later the interludes twice, 4 bars each, without instrumentation.
M. 326 [327?]:		The Dresden copy lacks the Clarinet, Bassoon and Horn staccato marks.
Mm.	352–354:	The MS lacks the Bass staccato marks (also m. 354 in Violin I/II).
M.	364:	The Dresden copy gives the Clarinets and Bassoons *sfp*. The MS lacks the Cello slur to the next bar.
M.	369:	The MS gives the Cellos another *piano*.
M.	384:	The MS lacks the Violin I staccato marks.
Mm.	385/386:	The Dresden copy lacks the Clarinet I slur.
M.	387:	The Dresden copy lacks the Clarinet and Horn slurs.
M.	388:	The Dresden copy lacks the Horn I slur (also on m. 398).
Mm.	405–407:	The Dresden copy lacks the Clarinet slur.
M.	408:	The Dresden copy lacks the first slur in the Clarinets.
Mm.	418–422:	The Clarinet markings, missing in the Dresden copy, are supplied from the Bassoon part.
M.	426:	The Dresden copy divides the Clarinet slur by half-bars (also in m. 428).
M.	430:	The Dresden copy lacks the Clarinet slur.
Mm.	439/440:	The Clarinet part is missing in the Dresden copy and is supplied here from the Berlin copy.
Mm.	451/452:	The MS phrases Violin I/II slur by whole bars.
Mm.	456/457:	The Dresden copy lacks the Horn [Trumpet?] I tie (also in mm. 462/463).
M.	459:	The Violin I slur is supplied from m. 453.
M.	506:	The MS lacks the Viola slur.
M.	512:	The MS lacks the Bass slur.
M.	514:	The MS lacks the Violin I/II slur.
M.	522:	The MS lacks the Violin I/II staccato marks.
M.	609:	In the MS, the Violas have e^1-g^1 on the 3rd and 4th quarters instead of g^1-e^1 as here.
M.	619:	The MS gives the staccato mark only in the Violin I part.
Mm.	629/630:	The staccato marks are supplied.
Mm.	644/645:	The Viola slur is altered on the basis of mm. 636/637.
Mm.	648/649:	The Dresden copy lacks the Horn and Trumpet ties here and in mm. 652/653.

Berlin-Wilmersdorf, Summer 1941

GEORG SCHÜNEMANN
KURT SOLDAN